Redemption Rain

poems

Jennifer Rahim

We acknowledge the support of the Canada Council for the Arts for our publishing program. We also acknowledge support from the Government of Ontario through the Ontario Arts Council.

Canada Council for the Arts Conseil des Arts du Canada

ONTARIO ARTS COUNCIL
CONSEIL DES ARTS DE L'ONTARIO

Cover Photo: webphotographeer/iStockphoto
Cover Design: Peggy Stockdale

Library and Archives Canada Cataloguing in Publication

Rahim, Jennifer, 1963-
Redemption rain / Jennifer Rahim.

Poems.
ISBN 978-1-894770-70-5

I. Title.

PR9272.9.R34R43 2011 811'.54 C2011-901131-X

Printed and bound in Canada by Coach House Printing

TSAR Publications
P.O. Box 6996, Station A
Toronto, Ontario M5W 1X7

www.tsarbooks.com

Contents

Earthquake Inventory

Earthquake 2010

Tuesday Jan 12: 2.30 p.m.

Before the earthquake rocked
Port-au-Prince with more fury
than an autonomic bomb,
BW 610 from Port-of-Spain
was safely on the ground
and my sole shake down
was from a customs officer,
young, hardened by his job,
who asked me twice
if I had anything
that was not in Canada before.
Each time I answered,
"No, sir," to a question
that struck me as an anachronism
in an age of travel
and oddly strung for a country
that flags its cosmopolitanism
like a religion.
He was bent on a confession
so on the third round
I thought hard of the contents
in my single roll-on,
then admitted, like a revelation:
"One coconut fudge, two
toolums and a sugar cake,
pink," and added, "I mean candy,"
sensing the qualifier
was necessary.

Winter entered his eyes
at my declaration.
They were the sweets of home,
a small comfort I allowed myself,
but an entire history
that travelled with me;
one I shared with the Guyanese woman
in trendy metropolitan wear
who sat taciturnly in 12C
guarding a phantom ascendancy,
and the elderly Trinidadian man
a few rows forward
in a grey fedora
and black leather coat
he never removed—
already feeling the cold.
It was this history
that had given me an Islamic name
the officer pronounced with a long *e*
then looked quizzically
from my face to my ID—
9/11 reruns terrorizing
his hidden screen.

When tectonic plates,
began secretly negotiating
their catastrophic shift,
the officer was asking,
"How much did you pay
for your candy, miss?"
I said, after a pause, "Three dollars,"
and to defuse what I caught
of his doubt injected,
"That is Canadian."
He stamped me in, then,

with no further question
understanding fully
that his currency
would be worth much more
than that of the islands, places
where the sugar in my sweets
made rum, hot countries
where people could escape
to roast their limbs on beaches
like the barbeques
of pillaging buccaneers,
only browning themselves
for their own tropic feast
like commercial cannibals.
He needed nothing more
and like a believer
in the dogma of his salvation
he accepted that the money
of the place I was from
could crumble and fall
like the frail shanties
of Port-au-Prince. Cathedral,
Presidential Palace and all—
rent like a judgement.
Everywhere rubble, white dust
like an upturned sepulchre.

3.35 p.m.

A grave:
it was the image that came
when I tugged my luggage
off the Airport Rocket,
journeying the cheapest way

and paying three Canadian,
the price of my candy,
to get first to Kipling,
the western end of the subway
that recalled the injurious poet
whose verses pined for *Home*,
a West of light and faith,
being sentenced to a hellish India
in the season of good cheer.
Heaven, believe me, is a location.

So coming from my south
with the undeclared slices
of my mother's black cake,
that had never been in Canada before,
safely stowed away
in Brazilian leather
(a bargain from a Rastaman
on Fredrick Street
who called to me on Christmas Eve,
"Sis, a small sale please
to buy something nice
for the youth man"),
when I saw the powdered tiles
of Kipling, the thought rained on me:
ash, the traffic of winter.
The merger was unexpected,
sudden, that exiled adjective
of good writing,
but native to my climate
with its hasty sunsets
and abrupt downpours,
temperaments I had marked,
undisturbed, as signs of home
until a lady, who stood next to me

under the eaves of *Kentucky*
on Independence Square,
looked up at a post-noon
apocalyptic sky and uttered,
"That is signs. Not a warning
and look at this rain."
We both had no umbrellas
and were in the same boat—
"stranded," I thought,
before she gave me a flyer
advertising a crusade in Couva.
I watched her walk on water
across Broadway, a new convert
exorcised of an old faith
that made no provision for hell.
I watched the canals swell
and felt a little like Peter
in need of a hand; but sinking
seemed a truer end
than being haunted by readiness,
anticipating a day that will come
as suddenly as August rain.

3.45 p.m.

The earthquake was a nightmare
tossing in Haiti's consciousness
when my train sped
to Castle Frank and the woman
I first saw on the Rocket
filed past
in search of a seat,
though the carriage
was half empty.

She dragged her duffle bag
behind her like a corpse.
I remembered she was last
to board the bus
and had said something softly
in her Créole to the driver
who didn't or couldn't answer,
but had waved her in
with defensive impatience.
I saw her that second time
on the train whose final stop
was Kennedy;
I saw her lumbering
in the direction of its thrust
like someone climbing a hill.

4.50 p.m.

It must have struck
as I boarded the No. 65 to Parliament.
I entered behind
two knapsack-toting teenagers
plugged into their iPods
and nodding their heads
to private rhythms
with the zoned-out look
of deliberate disconnect.
I too put on the wide-angled gaze
of public commuters
as the bus rattled along a street
named after its buildings
in the third year
of Toussaint's rebellion:
the time of a different split,

for Canada. We suffer
our differences
unequally.
So as I walked east
towards the Distillery, in six below,
with my *embark* rumbling
in my wake like a wounded love,
taking the cold
after a brief respite
from staying with the bus
as it swung west on Front
then doubled back
along the Esplanade's decent poverty,
I thought only of the *jadda*
fenced by thin plastic bags.
Distrusting the automated street stops,
she had made a ritual of half
standing at intervals, bowing
forward as Muslims do at prayer
to see ahead of her,
afraid of missing her stop—
the soiled fringes of her dress
far more streetwise.
Then at Parliament and Queen
she stood, frozen, a stranger
to what should have been familiar.

5.26 p.m.

When at last I switched on
the blessed heat,
then the TV and heard:
"My God, the world is coming
to an end," and saw the cloud

envelop Port-au-Prince,
the *jadda's* rehearsed plea,
"Please, let me off!"
her panic bypassing the bell,
resounded like an aftershock.
200,000 dead
and a pastor with the faithless
tongue of new grief lamented,
"Haiti is a cemetery."
Horrible, in any language,
sounds the same.
Yes, there is a world
that must end and Haiti,
our first light, is now
its grim apocalypse
as Obama's slick neighbourliness
slouches to its long-injured soil
with an unholy advent shrouded
by the stench of death
and provoked desperation
as pregnant carriers arrive
like Trojan horses with arms
empty of real need.

This is not a time
for sleep. Not now,
when the evil Toussaint fought
and fights, resurrects its head
like Revelation's cosmic beast
with might to sweep
the very stars from heaven.
This is the time
Carter portended, when dreams
must birth again, revolution
for Haiti,

misused child
of our freedom, lies helpless
at the very door
of the dragon's jaws
and her betrayal
is already our condemnation.
Hell, believe me,
is also a position.
That is why Robertson,
that deluded evangelist,
could preach the devil freed,
then cursed Haiti,
as though the will to liberty
must seek absolution
from what withholds
its very freedom.

Wednesday Jan 13: 11.21 a.m.

Trinidad called to say
that in St Augustine,
where the literati gathered
to honour Walcott,
Rudder's penitent prayer,
Haiti I'm sorry,
opened the proceedings,
pleading for all our abuses,
demanding reparation
for your losses
from a Caribbean
that moves on
the strength of your steel.

Even here, Aiyti,
I see the kaleidoscope

of your makeshift tents stretched
like a quilt of solidarity
that shames us, silences
our insipid religion
and hand-out politicking.
I see each hoisted square,
an SOS to winged ancestors
who stormed you free
of Napoleon's twisted heaven.
They will not now
deny you presence.
You are the best in us
we too must save
lest we all die
bankrupt of spirit
while the spangled stars
rule our fate.
If poetry means anything,
let this be a mouth charged
like Jeremiah's call to build
with much more resolve
the temple we too dimly
dream ourselves.

Haiti

For the earth has spoken,
to you, her magma Creole.

Full-throated syllables, up-
rising from deep down,

an honest elocution—
rudimentary sound: guttural

nouns, forthright, strong,
the rumbled conviction of verbs

unfettered by reticence
as the first poetry of creation.

A secret has passed between you
so wonderfully terrible,

it laid your cities prostrate,
raptured your citizenry.

Now, we look to your remnant
courtesy cable TV

and garble theories thinking
ourselves saved.

Only the wise among us pin
our ears to the ground,

listening in hope of catching
even a half syllable

of the language forming
like a new world on your tongue.

Earthquake Inventory

7.0: 8.8: 6.4. They say calamity comes in threes. *Then what?* Tears. Lamentations. Repairs. 12th: 7th: 3rd. Some days we remember by want we have lost. *Is it all grim?* Limbs. Houses. Lives. 230,000: 700: 0. Suffering, some say, on any scale, is never a numbers game. *But isn't zero neutral—it evens everything.* That's precisely the point. *Anyhow, there's another loss for the record. It now takes 1.26 millionths of a second less to complete a day.* Is that right? *Sure, we've been robbed of time.* Was it ever ours?

An Ode to SPAM

If this were a poem,
I would call it
"An Ode to SPAM"
and I would write it,
praying the cadence
of each syllable
as Neruda
must have done
when deep-tutored by gratitude
he sang the praises
of the ordinary.
If this were a poem,
I would write of those weeds
among my e-mail
like maybe Whitman wrote
the divinity of grass
or maybe, like Goodison,
pray a rosary of their names.
Oh yes, if this were a poem,
I would bless all
owners of bogus addresses
and contemplate their messages
like sacred texts:
those hard to resist offers
to reap retirement millions
sent by imaginatively
challenged spammers
all desperate to unload
massive inheritances
or siphon off dormant accounts
as though conspiring

to spread abroad the lie
that Africans are scammers;
not at all like their UK neighbours—
still high on civility
they announce unsolicited
winning lotteries
for a small trade in identities.

Then there are those files
labelled *confidential*
promising the revelation
of amazing details
once you click attachments
that are really neuroses
of every persuasion
masquerading as viruses;
and, of course, among these,
are those invitations
to misadventures in desire
and the offer of aids
to enhance pleasure
from folks in dire need
of mental quarantine.
Seriously now,
if this were a poem
named *Ode to SPAM*,
it would weep
uncontrollable buckets
as over a much-loved city.
It would lament blindness
and predict apocalypses.
It would pour each message
into a sacrificial cup
and bid you

Come, drink forgiveness
and live.
But this is not a poem;
and frankly, some things
are better flagged
UNREDEEMABLE
and swiftly dispatched
to languish
in junk-mail
HELL.

Going Grey

It comes around like the seasons:
the romance with going grey.

One morning you declare a fast
from all manner of hair dyes.

Good-bye L'Orèal, Dark and Lovely,
Clairol, and all their kind.

Unfriendly chemicals, discoloured
pillow slips, beauty salon bills,

and those miscalculated spills—
all seem such vanity.

So like a neophyte drunk
on zeal you banish

your last touch-up kit
not wanting to risk relapses.

Your mission: total surrender
to the hard-sale grace of aging:

the distinguished look of grey:
the proverbial wisdom display.

For one or two weeks, you spend
a precious portion of the morning

considering the change and think:
silver is really lovely—indeed!

By the third, when it is clear
you've been secretly multiplying

the silver, doubt slips in:
is this really necessary

for one's sense of integrity—
this public display of age?

But you hold strain believing,
I'll soon grow into it;

and in the interim, like a budding
heretic you explore options:

the comb forward rule offers
an indulgence as you consider

the advantages of visors, head-
ties, hats, even wigs.

Then, mercifully, you hit upon
the wonders of waterproof mascara,

which is not cheating—merely
buying time to brave the crossing.

By the fourth week,
your resolve is in jeopardy.

Officially diagnosed
with *re-growth syndrome,*

you contrive to stay at home
finding evening more tolerable.

To make matters worse,
you've been noticing people

are staring at your hairline. Others
politely avert their eyes and friends,

with the kindest urgency, whisper:
time for that touch-up, my dear.

By the fifth week or so,
the catechism of waiting fails

and you discover yourself
a brief convert to going natural.

After all, *self-honesty is a far cry*
from surrendering to a little dye

and, with a clear conscience,
recommit to the cover-up creed.

Hair-wise, at any rate, silver,
too, may be just a style.

To be sure, there are a hundred ways
to wear one's wisdom.

To be sure, there'll be more seasons
for courting conversions.

It's all a personal matter anyway—
how we choose to journey
                                        down.

Teaching Poetry a Little Dyslexic

for the class of 2010

DISCLAIMER: I take no responsibility for abducted verses. They were in the air and I welcomed them. My motto is this: All's fair in love and poetry

Signs arrive,
troublesome reversals
getting even *poews* wrong.
Words misbehaving, flicking
away correctness. Badmind.
WORDS. Concrete
image-rants
    aGAINST
de ORder
to write
    in metre,
breath wide as history
raging against Iambic-
Miss
DIS
MIS-
    ORDER

to master English metre

wanting spondaic CUSS OUTS
Jump Up   shouts
or
just a little trochee trip
JOU-VAY

chipping
down de road—
   JOU-
VAY
   no lame foot mode.

By this time it was clear
POERTY
   is a MUTANY.

   Language rioting,
colluding its In-CLU-sion,
like during that STRESS lesson
when a typo demanded
I read the CLU(e)
and free-up the session
for words were in rebellion,
brewing CA CA-CA
CA-COPHONY
(a second year
at failure to pronounce
correctly
the chaos of sound)

Yes, even my tongue
chose disobedience—

imagine: teaching
the "rules" of F—R—E—Eeeeeeeeeeeee
eeeeeeeeeeeeeeee VERSE
(misperformed air quotes
upstaged by unintended rabbit's ears
or maybe a plea
for PEACE:
     write as you want

whatever you want
        Pleeeeeeeeeeeeeeee-
ease)

then the unexpected plunge
while reading Neruda's praise of socks
saw then said
canyons for *cannons*
wanting, beyond consciousness,
those armoured feet
to travel deep,
walk gently
        unshod
to the very heart
of the earth's beat.

O the signs were there,
gone clear—the Keatsian black out
on *beauty* spotted, thankfully,
by the Account-returnee,
fresh from England.

Glo-ri-ous paradoxes
colonizing logic:
Mama D'glo's migration
to the ocean—salt and freshwater friendly
like any self-respecting hybrid.

O Trouble was out,
and like good haunts
WORDS
came floating in that learned air,
the way inspiration often comes—
unannounced:

"I have problems with scansion,"
Joey confessed.
"Welcome to the club,"
I said, levelling the scale—
identifying—"a little,"
he inquired,
          "dyslexic?"

I didn't get the mix
but the message carried well—
my mathematical fumble
that rubbed the cinquain
two whole syllables,
Course Outline date tangles
and then, like an anamorphic nightmare,
in November,
                    in November my dears,
even with Disney, Poe &
Christie upstairs
putting in a prayer for me,
portfolio submissions leapt
into two thousand and eleven—
the only "error" (I confess)
that went really well,
got them imagining:
what if,
          what if
with matter-season approaching
in anaphoric November,
          what if

there were twelve more months
to perfect rebellion.

So in spite of (ellipses disallowed)
poetry was going on—
the inevitable had come,
hearts *flat-lined* by obsessive forms
revived
changed
like that incredible bajhan triolet
that came my way
its mantric hymn
believe
believe
believe
advancing
like a new faith
or
like when *polished feet*
find their wings
FLY

B O L D

releasing

dead things

making poetry

truly
ALIVE

Caught

One night in the middle
of reading, her mind hooked
on some cryptic phrase,

its decipherability
shimmering under the surface,
like the trail of phosphorous

a fish leaves before vanishing,
returning to its deep, but
in that showing makes a mark

that marries the heart,
gone, without ever going
had without ever having.

So she remained harnessed
to the strain, her whole being reeled
in or hauled out to that wonder,

she could not decide which,
only that wanting was a light
eclipsed only by a language

that tugged her fathoms
beyond herself, from herself
approaching its depths.

Killing Saddam

(Miami, 2002)

i

Poems come
in-between
the living daily-
bread
congestions
net-
working
futures
as headline news
re-
runs

WAR

democratic gun-
talk, white
house
breathing
termination.

They come
a seeing
            or brief
grace to rip the veil

un/real
the screen-
playing

op liberation in Iraq. Tanks
and troops—stars!
in Baghdad, city
of thieves
Arabian night
stories

SHOCKing
in the dark
          death glows
     beautiful

AWEsome
an emerald sky
halos
a thousand innocents
blasted free
for one sad
damned man

But the Euphrates runs on
through Babylon

Silent
evolution
renames
     the beast.

ii

I sit watching in a room
made for transit—
idyllic a.c. comfort
and smiling service like the brochure-
holidays from where I came.

In the belly of this war machine
there is a kind of peace,
except on TV.
A newscaster's toasted face
mimics Middle Eastern heat.
Fluoride teeth flash victory,
talk rains of rocket sorties,
guided missile accuracies,
POW Lynch rescued a thousand
and one times over
and over again
as if to right
the unnamed Iraqis dead.
Nation-lips smack
as after ice-cream.

I never knew death
tasted so sweet.

iii

I scream
a small sound
(not loud)
amid CNN featuring
allied force
        feeding
democracy
to children
eating shrapnel like cereal
faces not so happy
as those tasting
Good Morning America
on the Fruity Loops AD,
nothing is better

than waking up
to the beautiful ones
born free
to name the wrong
their right to batter.

I scream a small sound
like a child's anguish
for limbs
scattered like seeds
across the battlefield

not loud
as soldiers whoo-haaing
after explosions
not loud
as the Egyptian youth shouts
"I hate Bush!"
in every living room
across the globe
his rage turning
a turning
burning

beauty
ripe

as ready seed.

iv

here
in the boot of a nation
kicking hard
like an infant
against its fears

warring
at the weakness of flesh
no technology
                no super currency
no God
could shield

our Caribbeans
are only so-free

I meet you
on this extension
of ourselves

coming from my wars
I bring you
my dead
unnamed ones
          trailing
my way
            like the unbaptized
seeking welcome

I bring you
this flesh
my Babylon
unsurrendered
to herself
I gather my skeletons
one by one
call after my lost ones
like the Iraqi woman
shouting after her dead son
"Answer me,"
wearing her long grief
among the rubble

crying,
"I am your mother
answer me,"
as though love
could wake the dead

I take off my shoes

now

when the stars
fall over Baghdad
without mercy
for the holiness of flesh

I bring you
my dead

v

We walk
the foot of Florida,
far
from any war
tourists
in a state selling
sunshine
vacations
packaged like islands
trade in beaches
Jolly Roger cruises,
Calypso and natives mixed
like Happy Hour
rum punches
Only in Miami

life is real
as on any screen
not a two week get-away
trip
from ordinary days

here

in spite of sunshine,
bananas courtesy Chiquita,
Latino and Soca vibrations
rocking down cosmopolitan
Bayshore,
Arrow feeling hot hot hot
the number one hit, still—
Miami
is a serious place
so real
the sea has swallowed many
who live beneath its heel
thirsting for a chance
to live
in this better place,
the foot in the belly
of the Caribbean Sea,
land of dreams
where men sport their nationality
on TV—
tiny flags
like a smear of something
eaten hastily
or in secret
now plain
for all with the eyes
to see
the foot in the mouth
of democracy

War Report

(Toronto, 2010)

Headlines again: Canadian
soldiers sold on patriotism
are dying in Afghanistan.

The officer, casuality151,
was a hero to his sisters
and loved like any son.

To be reported dead at 24
is anywhere a tragedy:
to be murdered by war.

To support troops and not
their mission betrays reason
to a blind spot.

An equivalent: to mourn
without memory of the more dead
in their own country.

Cataclysmic will be the failure
to grant even grief
its full democracy.

Talking History

The No. 64 (northbound)
strains along its route
as CTV runs its clip
of a Stetson-clad retiree
flying an Anglo-Canadian flag
somewhere in New Brunswick,
the place known best, by me,
for its tinned sardines;
but French Canada is peeved
as old Acadian wounds smart.

My host explodes,
That's so right wing!

I decline responding
and I simply think,
Oh, an intercolonial
squabble.

The silence bristles
and I reap an unsolicited
history lesson:

Do you know about the Acadians
and the Great Expulsion?

My history fails me.

The British kicked them out
and stole their land—
Now this again. It's so unfair!

I deep breathe centrally cooled air,
my gaze glued to the screen.

That's the history of Canada.
It was born at the point of a gun.

Something in my head clicks.

The truth about colonialism,

I begin, measuring my words
the way, I learnt, immigrants
first navigate space,

is that it affected people
differently.

But Canada was never a colony—
not for long at any rate,

my host interrupts,
thinking the fact
necessary.

Sure, I say,
concepts can be as shifty,

glancing at the Emily Carr print
mounted on the wall
and barricaded by the sofa.

(When I arrived
I was told it was a favourite:

majestic Haida totems
made to honour dead chiefs thrust
against the ceiling.)

History doesn't simply
let you off at the next stop.

What exactly are you getting at,
my friend?

Just then the flag dispute
story ends
and the channel flicks faster
than a flipped page
shifts an age.

Midnight Robber

Imagine, meeting *him*
at St Lawrence Market
on Front and Jarvis!

It was cold February—
Saturday evening,
shortly before closing.

Shoppers were frisky
and smiling, content
from reaping bargains.

She, managing her purchases,
stood amid the bustle
contemplating peaches.

Her silvers and coppers hung
like a small weight
on her arm.

Settled on the merit of the deal,
she proceeded to extract the sum
for the cost of three

when her purse gave way
and a wild cosmic shower
rained down.

LORD more than she exclaimed,
and as she knelt
in the market's heavy traffic

trying to retrieve her change
she heard him—a voice
in her own language, chorusing:

name de hell yuh livin in;
name de truth yuh escapin.
Mortal dis is payback day!

She never saw a face
but being so low felt the hammer
of booted feet,

glimpsed the trail of a cape
with a coffin sailing in its wake.
Then, as though hearing a whistle,

she sprang to her feet
and hurried away like someone
who had been searching for stars

in the wrong place.

To a Believer Who *So* Fears the Dark

I confess it.
I sleep with my shadows,

no longer banishing in me
what is homeless.

I choose to befriend
my suffering self.

We wash together,
feast at the same table.

This I know
is what now separates us—

you with the sheep
and that (I suppose) leaves me

with what is left—the goats.
But I'm not complaining;

you see, I'm learning
to be happy with my lot.

No more crying
on your shoulders.

No more preferring
your side of heaven.

They (the goats, I mean)
are sure-footed beasts,

so I feel my high ascent
is guaranteed.

Goats (read shadows)
got a raw deal.

Sheep just happened to be
on the right side

of the street.
So that cancels the left.

Frankly, sheep-style
is too docile for me.

So I'll take my chances
on the mountains,

which is fine,
since falling is my business.

Don't be scandalized,
but the entire truth is

I have decided
to wed my darkness.

Honestly, I have no regrets.
Our talk is so full

of recognition, the light
we generate makes night, day.

No need to be afraid.
My advice is this:

wear UVR100 lenses
when next you look at me,

or else my light will be
the dark your naked eyes see.

I Mean

I am of the House named
Compassionate:

All Merciful: I mean Womb.
My name and God
make One.

And I, too, am
the Unnameable One
the altar

where God is reborn
again, and *that* is
my sure salvation.

Not a nobody:
the one to turn your back on.
I am the All you hold un-free.

I am everybody's race.
Everybody's faith.
Everybody's love and hate.

I refuse nothing you give me.
I grow here: walk that beach:
swim that sea: climb that tree.

I am the woman
in that J'ouvert band,
dancing her rhythm.

Wednesday:
I put ash on my face
and eat the Undead Bread.

Once I played a convent mas'.
More than once I tried
to run from poetry
and this, I hear,
is not only my journey.

Once I slept beneath
the thunder of a drum.
When I woke up,
it was day
and I could speak
my spirit-names.

More than once I loved—
well, that is a long story.
The short is—I love,
eternally.

One day I went quite south
to ask poetry
why it chose to die.

Now I know
that is not a question
you ask an ocean.

Since then I sleep
with sea in my ears.
I meet the dead without fear.

I am from this place
and I expect you will treat me
no different
from those who belong,

here. I know one thing:
I am your offering
and you *will* deal with me.

And that, too, is love.

A Hunting Story

i

There is a way a life pursues you: not
as, you imagine, a hound trailing
your scent, a howling bent on finding you,
at end, cornered and crazed like some terror-
struck agouti praying the hunter's gun,
as in Dominic's tale, fails to fire,
not once, but twice—the chance to escape what
pursues you like a love-sick Apollo
set on possession—the reason Daphne
chose to die and be born again a tree.
Better to birth the leaves that garland bards
than live interned in another's heaven.

So, Dominic, what if that pommerac
in which you sat sentry, concealed, and saw
that agouti come to feed at twilight
was converted Daphne's southern sister,
and she jammed your too eager trigger so
the beast and you could then see each other
before released to run free, the feral
fiction of encounter sweet on your tongue,
the God you want and do not want to tame,
that primal thing, unhoused, crick-cracking in
your veins, ready words wanting expression
like when Jack Mandora shout
                                        and story jump out.

ii

And that is what is meant by being found
by heaven's hound—the gift of naked look
and fecund sound, the mischievous word
that slips and falls on those bastard apples
gathered on the ground to break the back
of every sentence, bringing blessed air,
fresh as the forests you love, worship pure
as Justin's uplifted arms, his fingers
mimicking the ecstatic dance of leaves,
his psalm a single elastic word sung
as simple recognition: B-R-E-E-Z-E

iii

Dominic, I am destined to returns
like a nun vowed to her heart's slow office
reciting the alphabet of her faith,
chiming scripture's familiar lines until
light breaks upon the page and makes a feast
of ordinary time as only prayer,
like air, can sanctify the common rhyme.
If poetry is my fate, *it* will yet
make an honest woman of me, teach me:
first, fidelity to the real, the field
where the miraculous lies hushed, at ease,
hidden from the careless eye that fashions
epiphanies as believers unfit
for waiting venerate invention starved
of the labour that ripens green days to myth.

iv

The truth is not one but two agoutis
came at dusk to feed as you sat atop
that pommerac unarmed, a spectator
to the sport that answered what cried in you
for veneration. "Is just a man thing,"
you said, "a kinda calling inside there."
It was the heart you struck. "Get it racing."
I knew, then, hunting was a salvation
and my judgement tripped on that desire
to protect something vital in yourself:
"Is a feeling fellars take drugs to get."
Again you struck your chest and silence fell.
In some distant cell, a phantom third beat
on a penitent's breast broke your spell.

v

I wanted repentance when forgiveness
was not your need—simply doxology:
the shoulder shrug from the hunter stationed
a branch down when the gun renounced the hunt
and left you hung as beasts fed on fallen
new world apples and silently moved on;
then, descending like demoted gods
you ran pell-mell through pitch dark to meet
a serpent in your path—its eyes mirrored
fear. "Yuh boy jump back about ten whole feet.
Only bush could make a big man do that."
I chewed on your raw theology,
a sceptic at the altar of the tale
that had made you the forest's disciple.

vi

My friend,
so much has passed
between us,
so much history
lived too carefully,
travelling our lines
dutifully upright,
like the strict penmanship
of my childhood
under Miss Julia's watch,
her Levitical ruler righting
the hand she pronounced
the devil's disciple.
Through the long dark
and mourning wear
of Toronto's winter,
I think of those beasts,
no doubt a couple, arriving
in the cool of evening
to feast unburdened
by garden myths, unsuspecting
even of your bogus aim,
for it was you that held the gun
in the second telling
of your tale that day
when you came to measure
for iron rails
to make walking safe.
As the tape slipped along
the stairway's crooked contours,
I wondered why
you had altered that detail
and then tried to correct it:

"The gun empty! Like the man feel
is he I woulda shoot
from the damn tree."

I understood then
you wanted me to see you
as capable of meeting
your target.
I watched you spring back
as you mimed the hit,
the act reframing for me
your run-in
with the fabled snake
that reversed your flight,
and I wondered
who first saw it, whose fear
had leapt the air.
But we moved on, talking
distractedly of the sea
and its salt.
"Everything bow to that,"
we agreed,
and you bottled water
from the seasonal stream
that neighboured my property.
"For the birds," you said.
"No chlorine—make them
sing sweet."
You had made a sideline
of selling them.
"Hard times. Everything
is business these days,"
you added quickly
like a plea.
"Sure," I said

and through that moment's gate
you rifled,
"Spare ah man a call—
from up there."
I had mentioned
my departure.
I nodded
and watched you,
sure-footed,
hurriedly ascend
Sheldon's botched stairs,
without fixing a price
for the railings.

So we parted,
each, in a way,
preserved from fault,
only a little undressed
like proprietors of an Eden
never tested, leaving only
the ripening mystery
of those two wild agoutis.

Redemption Rain

A Simple Honesty

I have always wanted to pray
my island with lips
kissed by flame.

I have always wanted to speak
its litany of names
in morning cadences—

hushed
like waves shuttling
night-washed sand.

I have always wanted to hear
those ancient tongues pronounce
their geography of homes,

each known by mountain
and river, forest and bird,
shape and blossom—and salt.

O for the mercy
of that unaffected alphabet.

I have always wanted
an earth: an island: a God:
in whose name

I, too,
am a simple honesty.

A Poem for Everyday

All poems must mean Sunday,
must be rest, itself,
not sleep.

A poem
must be awake
or else it cannot speak.

Never a dream—
though it could be,

a poem must be
what touch can feel
and sight can see.

A poem
is fullness—
what Sabbath truly means,

when time is eternity—
yesterday and today,

present as the earth is
what it means to be,
after God, simply, mystery.

A poem is an island—
never singular
or complete.

No, it is always neighbour,
always community.

To know it,
is to name what is there—

the wise always baptize
with their eyes.

See: Hear: this poem is
so much more

and nothing but itself—
like an island
that means rest.

A Creed for Mornings

I believe
in the advent of new light,
the ordinary mercy of green,
the quiet generosity of soil
and the benediction of breeze.

I believe
in the belly-comfort of a cup
cradled in my palms each morning,
in the first thanksgiving sip
of coffee or tea—
for taste too is sacred.

I believe
in standing before sea
or mountain
or familiar backyard chaos
and savouring long
the wonder of flavours
in ground bean or drawn leaf:
that, too, is contemplation.

I believe
my temple or church,
my mosque or palais
is the place I most want to be,
the altar where my spirit is free:
a mere witness to generosity.

I believe
in the veneration of things small,

especially those within,
and if ever I make a good confession,
it will be of my failure
to welcome in
the beginning
of new-born mysteries.

I truly believe
pure religion is the full-measured,
pressed-down devotion
to their secret becoming.
So praise be
every mother of these.

I believe
the only prayer worth praying is this:
God please make me
an acre of ground
where all manner of seeds—
the born-and-grow ones,
those that make hard sea
or sky journey to here or there,
the ones that come from strange,
never-before graft, those in doubt,
and even the drop-about—
can begin the business
of dying and rising
that makes for good trees.

Every seed is an orphan
until a patch of soil
agrees to house it.
So I believe
the first holy communion
is when earth and root make one.

That is when the slow
and right ascent
to spread-wide-giving begins.
Trees, if you believe me,
are the first gods.

This is why at every dawn,
I believe,
it is right and proper
to give due praise
to the Eternal Sower of good seed
who delivers harvests
of spill-over living
and the simple consolation
of a familiar warm
and friendly cup.

Blessing

If out of the blue,
bird-drop stay jus-so

and fall on you,
don't wipe it off.

Never mind the *A-A*
that jump from your mouth,

make you stand dead
on spot, when touch, warm

like fresh-lay-egg hit home.
Let that utterance be

like when a language reach
and shake-up old speech.

If one bright morning,
sky-messenger

swifter than eye-catch
rain on you

even though the sky
turn-off her water

and cicadas bawl 'til they blue,
welcome the blessing

with an *Ahh*—release
that call open-arm praise tree
into being.

Storehouse of Names

i

How to write the scripture
of simple things
when the very shadow

of a deity labours unseen
beneath the green wood
of the ordinary?

Already the question trips
on its self-consciousness, already
the shy sacred takes flight

from this crude crucifixion of lines
aspiring to be a benediction
to the mercy of time.

Where does one begin?
if not with the litany of origins,
and its storehouse of names:

I come from an island
named Iere, after the quick-
winged messenger of the Sun Father.

It hums as it travels, so great
the joy of spreading rebirth.
Some believe the birds are spirits

of dear departed souls
come back from the hereafter
to deliver tall instruction

or with their celestial plumage,
delight the grounded.
Columbus called them *flying jewels*,

the self-same misguided traveller
who baptized my landscape
with the eternal mystery

of community, *La Trinity*—
the very lesson his legion of ships
could not learn fast enough

to spare an entire race
the sacrilege of a monstrous greed
not even Colibri could outspeed.

So in the *Book of Shame*
it is written that ten thousands
of birds were slaughtered to appease

the god of fashion when a robe of skin
reserved for Taino priests
gained the pope's wardrobe.

Cesaire, that prophet of returns,
rightly saw *contact* as the absent level
in Colon's vulgar vision.

No gateway to El Dorado,
that dream province of avarice,
it chapels the *Chronicle of Salt*

whose creed is forgiveness
and is home of high priest,
                    Lovelace.

ii

I repeat it now, differently:
how does one begin a prayer
to the ocean's infinite mercy?

How to begin its practice
with no clear footpaths for returns,
only echoes of near

and distant loves that haunt
the ports through which we came—
captor, enslaved, indentured,

all of us seeded in crossings
and born again in the fount
of forgotten names.

This is the sea's retribution.
It makes no prodigal returns
to find a home left

waiting at the heart's gate,
like love will always
wait.

It harbours no confessor's memory
of a too-hard love of there,
offers only the miracle of arrival.

How do I pray
the sacrament of those who stay
where surf preaches

the long sermon of meetings,
and Africa, India too,
is that neighbouring horizon,

not a hemisphere away,
but just over there, east
of every beginning.

I will tell this one story
and I offer it imperfectly
on a page that walks a line

between land and sea,
until, mercifully, breakers
steal its small thunder,

and salt and reshuffle
its chapters to tell
greater fictions.

We come to the office
of islands where the knee bends
to honour the hours.

The last station will be
this sacred reading
at the water's edge,

where home never departs
but is a constant arrival on
the endless scroll of an ocean.

In the beginning
and the end will be
the tide's ritual migration

to and from a single line
where light draws and hurts the eye
and vision is an umbra

at centre, like the void
before every genesis,
not emptiness,

but where time
is a spectral dance of presences
in the dark before recognition.

This liturgy of water
and light, this pilgrimage
to the shrine of a horizon

will be the final solemnity—
the prayer at which I met Mervyn
that morning of his departure

from St Martin, an island
split between a French
and Dutch quarter,

its name a sacrament
on Taino tongues: *Sualouiga:*
Land of Salt,

invincible binder of demons,
talisman for evil spirits
that suck blood

and steal souls, mineral
that toughens skin, sting
that triggers sptifire, frees

limbs to run and coaxes
pots to surrender flavours
that revive flagging wills

or seduce the unsuspecting
to devour their ruin.
Blessed salt, preserver

against all manner of rot,
sacred healer of wounds
and stubborn afflictions.

I saw him that morning,
solitary, at a breakfast table
of a hotel whose name summons

the ocean and the invasion
that rouses agitated flesh
cloistered in shell to birth gems.

He sat facing generous windows
designed to let the sea in—
a hybrid's recall

of great houses and ships
as if the beauty of islands
must always be tethered

to the horror of their history.
He sat at the close of his meal
in adoration's hermetic calm,

with the usual litter of a free
continental breakfast before him—
nibbled too-dry toast, yesterday's

appearance of cheap jam and butter,
coffee going cold and the one
redeeming glass of juice

wishfully just squeezed
to complete the brochure tropics
of which even natives dream.

He was looking out to sea
from behind dark sunglasses.
I thought the view caused pain.

I was only half wrong.
It was peace that he savoured,
an earned surrender

to the consolation of place,
the way he wore his mother's ring
on his wedding finger,

its worn face, the shape
of a shield, the story of endurance
that love means

or the nakedness it yields,
as I saw him,
well-brushed by time,

wearing that infinitely
cherished thing, its meaning
clearer to me then

than his life's discipline
of sounding the soldered Creoles
of his landscape.

He sat filtering the whole deal:
his love of the sea and the sting
of unrelenting light.

To an island, the sea
is discovery like love's arrival
is always mystery

and so seduces the heart
to behold what it cannot fully grasp,
but finds in that gaze

the contemplative's path
where travel is what we do
to come to rest in the joy

of every sorrow, the gain
of every loss, as I saw him,
facing the sea, transported

by the tenderness of attention,
and I wanted him freed
of every hurt—

my too careless dismissal
of affection, the injury
to his hand from the jump seat

in the minivan as we loaded up
for St Philipsburg,
and I said aloud, half jokingly,

Let me heal you,
and he half-seriously
allowed me to hold his pain

between my palms,
not knowing what I wanted
was his forgiveness

for the pride of my youth,
and a womanhood too bruised
to be gracious.

We come, each in turn,
to our epiphanies. For me,
there will always be the sea

when I recall his whispered
affirmation: *You seem different.*
I laughed and said,

I hope you mean better.
He nodded. It was his season
of easy transparencies.

The way he confessed
his discomfort with eating meals
without meat—

a childhood stigma
he still carried.
It was a sign of poverty.

I glanced at the ring's
thinned gold and imagined
the mother he wanted close;

and when we parted
there was nothing
but the merciful shuttle
                    of an ocean.

Redemption Rain

I have been praying for rain—
relentless downpouring
like Mary's weeping
that Resurrection morning
when all that was love to her
was lost. O, that morning
was her hurricane of asking,
Who take him? Where they put him?
Not even a body left to touch.
Yes, I have been praying for rain
like that first Easter morning
when so much eye-water fall
it drown her world like Noah's.
To be sure, that dread morning
when she looked inside that grave
a womb-turn earthquake
rocked her world again
and bring-down-sorrow flow—
swept away the very image
of what she so loved in its flood.
O yes, I have been praying for rain
to end every dry season—
heart-water salted like Mary's
so love may speak redemption
with my name.

Saint of Glass Houses

O Mary, why would I ever want
to escape you, patron saint
of already shattered glass houses?

Today, a spammer offered me
a collector's deal
in assorted UK glassware.

What could I do with those?
Clay is my preference.
I like the idea of making art
with earth.

As you know, it's a tradition old
as the garden myth
even Jeremiah found hard to resist;

but I like to think the version
you show up in completes it—
never mind the dirt for clay alteration—

the principle carries. The medium
best suits us humans—something
to do with the remake option.

Once experienced,
working with glass is elementary—
it makes one unafraid of stones

thrown from any direction.

My Dear St Thomas

My dear Thomas,
saint we prefer not to imitate.
Who wants to be the one
branded *doubting* anyway?
It doesn't sit well with the pride
we take in announcing faith.
Being outside the chosen circle
is never ever comfortable.
What of that anyway—was it fate,
not being in the right place
that gave those others
a jump start on believing?
Or was it a way to teach
a different lesson?

O St Thomas, perhaps you had
the better part after all—
for to fully believe you pushed
at every decent border
to touch wounds you knew
well enough to name
until they became, for you,
a Saviour. Saint of what we believe
until we truly see, pray for us
that the unbelief our faith conceals
may match your honest doubt.

At Gethsemane

At Gethsemane he was alone
and with his friends.

It was a night
too heavy for watchfulness

so they slept
through his weeping. Tears fell,

the evangelist said, like *blood*.
Only the earth took him in,

drank without reserve his sorrow-
cup and asked for no favours.

What he really wanted
was the company he loved

while he talked
with the God of his heart.

But it was night and much too late
to bear his asking-cross.

He wept and only the olive trees
heard his suffering.

Still, all he wanted was love returned
in a small request: *Stay with me*.

But his friends were empty of words—
for grief—for fear.

So they took their rest
and dreamt a different end.

At the very last, an angel stepped in
and he drew strength.

He really wanted his friends;
but it was night and sleep came,

naturally.

Spare Change

We all have them—
leftover coppers of our spending

carelessly thrown into once-loved
jars or bowls, exiled

to an inglorious spot on the kitchen
counter's cultivated order.

Those time-dulled
or new-minted strays, stored

just beneath notice,
keeping company with the bits

and pieces of our living
that never quite make the garbage:

discoloured scraps
with their chaotic collages of names

and telephone numbers
like askew Sudoku puzzles,

orphaned buttons,
rubber bands, assorted twisters,

the perennial paper clip,
as if running short of what we need

to bind and shore-up things
were a secret phobia;

yellowing utility bills,
all stamped paid, but saved

past necessity—
just in case the system fails.

There is something we distrust
about the letting go of things,

even those bothersome coppers
with no real power to purchase,

holding on to them,
wary of that curse of wastage,

anticipating the moment
we may need that one black cent

to bail us out
of a half-expected hell.

Talking History Revisited

for Liz Rowley

Her verdict was this:
she had killed it,

the Amaryllis I had noticed,
last summer, but couldn't name—

it was too late for blossoms.
Leaves arched like emerald

spider's legs sunned themselves
in the kitchen's western window

where the light was a slow, furious
dying, mercifully filtered

by twin firs, evergreens, planted
at a beginning abandoned

but survived by love reseeded
with the names of children

now matured like those trees—
their new meaning.

We stood, friendly strangers,
in that January gloom,

mourners at the grave
of a naked pot

where the remnant bulb sat
with three more, like bombs.

The percolator, she confessed,
had steamed the plant to death.

It was an honest repentance
for misplaced guilt,

and I wondered at her
gardening amnesia,

why she felt contrition
was a place to begin;

and, in winter's softened light,
I saw again those living-

room totem poles, heard her disclosure
that she was from Vancouver,

the soil that must have seeded
defiance in her then rooted

her among the ranks, wedded
to fighting for liberties

my history could not,
at first, grant her.

Maybe it is always in the end
about the light, the way

we see each other;
so, I said, "Not to worry,

they'll revive. In the spring,
they will come alive."

It was a weak remedy
for all our follies

but it was the only absolution
I could give as we stood,

each a little exposed, agreed,
at least, to believe

that the Amaryllis will bloom
from those dormant wombs.

Mother.Laughing

It is so like her—
that readiness for laughter,
uncontrollable bouts
of waterfall happiness
that still irritates father.
"Forever giggling,"
he grumbles from the cloud
of his disapproval.
Now we smile easily
with each other
and move on—our way,
we think, of inviting him
to find another centre.

She tells her story like a god
drunk on her wild creations.
This one is about her trip
to the bank when this street-dweller
passes but then abruptly turns
and pursues her, calling
at the top of his voice,
"Shirley-Ann! Shirley.
Girl, is me!"
But she keeps a straight head
and hurries onward
like a fugitive.

I try to imagine her hustling
with that badly re-hinged ankle.
"So you didn't recognize him?"
I ask, only to fuel the tale.

"No," she says falling
over herself, laughing.
"All I thinking is people
watching me saying:
Now the man turn vagrant
she playing she don't know him."
I understood then
she was laughing at herself,
not her failure at recognition,
but that she still worried over
how people saw her.
"Is only when I reach Republic
and he say again, Shirley,
is me. Carlton."
She finally knew who he was.

"I say, Lord man!
What happen to you?
And, you know, after all that
the man smile. "
"Because you saw him," I said.
"But I didn't make him out,"
she repeated, wonder-struck.
"I only thinking people saying,
Look how she playing prim now
the man hit bottom."

It was *her* lesson
for the day—the way
we never really change.
I think that is how
she will die, laughing,
at her shortfalls
like a child.

Justin's Penguins

The sofa is his ladder up.
Small toes grip the backrest
as he hangs on my shelves
like a little Hanuman,
and with the hand
not anchored for balance
selects a text
before inching deftly left
to deposit his find.
I try to figure his logic
and decide it's the colours he's after—
those with the orange spines.
He's too young to string letters
though he can sing
almost all twenty-six
once he gets going.

My notice spurs him on.
This, he shows to complete
his asking.
A book, I say.
He repeats the word,
elated at the sound—I think.
Under Western Eyes
was no joy ride.
Conrad ends up between
my *Dictionary of Symbols*
and Fanon's *The Wretched*
of the Earth.
His untutored poetics
draws my smile.

His father comes in
just when he picks an Austin
and half-chides, *Justin, stop messing*
with your Auntie's shelves.
But he is hooked
by his mission and edges
resolutely to his station.
It's ok , I say. *Let him play.*
We watch him tuck *Emma* in—
his face a-light.

It's the Penguins,
my brother declares.

He sees my bewilderment.
He likes to look at them.
But his tone is a decibel
too tender, and I look at him,
Chris, my little brother,
bearing a man's pain
of promises shelved.
So we're thankful when he tires
of his game and descends
to tumble among the cushions.

When they're gone
and my study is again a cell,
I survey the damage
and discover rough notes
for a postmodern lecture:
my *Complete Shakespeare*
neighbours *Representing: hip hop*
culture and the production
of black cinema. Bettelheim's
The Uses of Enchantment sits

with my saved *West Indian Reader,*
and *100 Great House Plants*
takes root between the *Wide*
Sargasso Sea of Rhys
and Weedon's *Feminist Practice*
and Poststructuralist Theory.

Then, one shelf from the top
in the far eastern corner,
I find his Penguin stash:
all seven assorted titles
with the publisher's logo—
birds in uniform tuxedos
stand in perfect line.
I remember Senior's jab at them
for *exchanging wings for flippers*
and pray instead that Justin
will learn to climb
the skies by being faithful,
like those Antarctic tenants,
to the infinity
                    of a single egg.

Petition

for Henrietta Lacks, d. October 4, 1951

This is a petition
for the long overdue canonization
of Henrietta Lacks,
housewife and daughter
of a tobacco farming family
from Virginia,
who walked through death's door
and came out the other side.
She didn't need no welcome party.
She didn't have to slip past
St Peter's security.
Not that one, Mistress Lacks.
Her credentials come direct
from the one who know, personal,
the heart science of crossing over
and leaving behind at the same time.
She tell herself, "Thirty-one
is no proper age to die. No girl,
Not so! Now is ripe to start
higher order work."
To be sure, that Dr G
was a brace face thief.
Never had the common decency
to ask permission to take piece
of her own body
and, to add insult to injury,
proceed to sell the lady's cells
free-sheet.
Is so bad habits linger.

But Hennie decide, "God doh sleep.
I have greater harvest to reap.
More life to carry-on than my five."
So though it pain her to leave,
she let that cancer do its work
and wait for her time to reach.
So start the tale of her
Immortal HeLa Cells
that to this day refuse to die
but simply multiply
and multiply.
And let me tell you on the side,
the general complaint
is they have their own
colonizing mission.
Every cell that touch Henrietta
take her line.
So this is a petition
for her canonization.
Let her venerable name
join company with all proven
ancestors and saints.
Let there be a verse
invoking her protection
and cure from all manner
of viruses and diseases.
Let this be her story:
what was everlasting in her
she left behind as pure gift
in that Baltimore laboratory.
Praise be her generosity
for keeping never-ending faith
with life.

Lines to Fanon

Fanon, when language cancelled you,
you slipped from your skin, made yourself
a poet of the world to touch the stars
that were yours to behold. Poetry, the obeah
you worked to salt the bad faith mounted
in words to poison relations and distort
even the I-eye that gazes into its pond,
unable to die for love of that self,
                                        looking in.

But there are those who walk backwards
into their homes, leaving every evil
in the yard like dust shaken from their feet.
Brother, the world is as it is. Mostly, we live
to die like you were buried metres
inside the country of your dreams
until others ushered you
                                        further in.

Meeting Mel

i

"Will I know you after what—
fifteen years?"

"It's been that long.
I haven't been counting," she said.

"That's the age of my eldest.
Bright and she likes to write."

He laughed and cleared his throat.

ii

"Are you there?"

"I'm here.
So you never quit smoking," she said.

"How do you know?"
"Your voice—it's changed."

"Well, I wear glasses
and lost my hair."

"Don't worry, I dye mine," she said
and laughed too quickly.

iii

The meeting point was the ROM.
It was an autumn Friday
and almost too cold to be
without a coat.

She saw him first
but never missed his curls
and thought his silver frames
a good choice.
It was the first time
she really saw him paired.

iv

"Too damn long," he said
when they came together at the corner.
He never mentioned how she looked.

"Where can we go?"

He scanned the street
and seemed taller
purposefully looking over her.

"Come," he said, taking her arm.
"We have six seconds
before the change."

v

They crossed to east of Bay
as the pedestrian timer counted
in reverse.

St Patrick's Day

The plant came
on St Patrick's Day
when the city wore glitzy green
and temperatures warmed
on beer and whiskey.

It was something to see—
an Echeveria enthroned in glass
atop a shelf stacked
with island tales
that backed an ample window
facing north—
all the windows did,
as though gauging
a farther freedom.

Wonderful to see:
a transplanted succulent
seated in strong black soil
where ascetic roots feed
drought-wise leaves
that make a perfect rose.

No big miracle:
just an ordinary plant
set against a concrete grove
where no less richer earth
nourishes sparse green.

No great revelation:
just a robust flower

fit like immigrants
for survival.

A wonder, really:
a tropical hybrid,
far from its hemisphere,
neighbours a revived

Victorian quarter
that once spirited
an entire province.

She overlooks Corktown
and St Paul's Basilica,
a convert to her soil,
fine filaments exposed
as if distilling a world
where the shamrock too
is a scarce conversion.

Weather Talk

The meteorologist on the *Weather Network*
is ululating unseasonal highs,

sweeping cold fronts off the continent
and showing more skin than usual.

I believe the signs and recklessly
down dress a layer.

Later that day at St Joseph and Bay,
under a clear blue and high sky,

I professed my faith
in the barometer's ascent to spring.

My witness, a Guyanese man
from Newmarket, Ontario,

well-insulated in grey wool
and black leather,

side-glanced me and said,
"I'll go with you on that one,"

then crossed the street
in the hunched gait of winter.

Good Poetry

Some folks believe good poetry,
like good girls, should stay at home.

Not the *see-an'-doh-hear* type,
but those that play the game right—

mouth trendy themes—spin
tired rhymes—dance in time.

Once, I attended that church,
sat up front, had the best view

and blessing of the house—
not entirely an unworthy religion.

Writing from that pew,
gives poetry its first mission.

But there is something to be said
for sitting back, mixed in

with the multitude—fidgeting
and yawning, mishearing

and nodding, making faith
with partials as the sermon drones.

There begins training in long
and broad vision,

the baptism in variance,
the worship without mountains

that gives poetry its great heart.
And once in a while,

simply up and take flight
for the first poem was really a bird.

The view from above, the distance
apart, gives poetry its girth—
makes verse a map of returns.

Mango Diplomacy

for Keith Ellis

Landscapes
are what journey with us:

the myriad moods
of two seasons,

the lay of land, texture
of beach and leaf,

the visitation of breeze,
the taste each fruit yields—

their memory, the eternal
tenants of our senses.

So you brought me
like a metropolitan anancy

boiled yucca, guava
and sweet potatoes

direct from Cuba,
smuggled past an officer

salaried to watchdog
the errancy of immigrants

wanting to savour
the flavours of home;

and minutes before
while driving along Spadina

where we noticed street stalls
laden with mangoes,

in November, you regretted
not bringing me those.

But not yet starved
of islands I never asked

the variety you meant.
I imagine, now, Jamaican.

Then in July's plenty,
reading the *Star's* story

of a Virginia Pakistani
who drove twelve hours

and crossed a border
for a taste of Chaunsa mangoes,

before the season closed,
I think of you,

your wanting me to have
the fruits of home,

giving me the geographies
of your love

like sacraments to weather
my first Canadian winter.

I think of Mr Haider,
busted on his return

with his beloved Chaunsas
that refused the bland diplomacy

of borders, preferred
instead to declare themselves

and bless both sides
with their passing.

It was my first lesson
in revolution,

a word you believe
like a faith:

like Cuba: the heaven
you disbelieve,

her language
your heart's breviary.

I remember now the fruit
you forgot that day

and I never tasted,
those mangoes whose name

I regret not asking—now
lost to me, like a home.

Poetry's Country

The heart writes its own poetry
in any geography.

Treasures, but needs
no one slant of light

when verse becomes citizen
of every country.

In time, a rhythm will arrive,
unfettered as air;

in any climate, it will venerate
the cycles of green.

There is a verse that knows
no nationality though married

to the surf's metre,
vowed to its salted Creoles,

is companion to every syllable,
truly free—it speaks

the uncommon tongue
but is heard by each.

Even poetry has its Pentecost,
will rest where all is flame: blood.

One day, it will come: a wind
storming this house we wear

like a seamless garment
through all our fractured histories.